Co

Introduction

Chapter 1: Prepping Your Manuscript

Chapter 2: Setting Up a Book Template in InDesign

Chapter 3: Creating Chapter Files in InDesign

Chapter 4: Creating a Print-Ready PDF

Introduction

This book is designed to give you the basic information you will need to design a book in the world's most widely used print layout software, Adobe InDesign. The program is so versatile that it can be used for a variety of purposes, including digital media for ebooks and websites. By reading this book you will have a rudimentary knowledge of the inner workings of InDesign. The first project may take a while, since you will be learning to navigate the program itself. But once you have learned how create new files, flow text, assign font styles, place images, and publish your book, every other book you produce after that using InDesign will be a piece of cake.

At the time this book was written, I had been working in InDesign for ten years. You could say that I know the ins and outs of the program quite well. I started out using it for print publishing in a professional setting. About eight years ago, I started working in book publishing on a full-time basis, so having a good knowledge of book design programs like InDesign really helped out immensely. Now that I work with authors full-time, I design books for them, as well as perform other tasks associated with publishing. My hope is that by reading this book you will be able to understand the basics of how to create a book file that is ready for printing and publishing.

Innovations in the publishing world have made it easier to write and publish a book. With the rise of print-on-demand publishing, you no longer need to order a large volume of books to make publishing worthwhile. In fact, the books are stored on a computer and created as soon as they are ordered. This efficient system has allowed millions of people access to publishing that hadn't existed before. And it has placed high demand on platforms that allow people to publish their own books.

By following the steps in this short ebook, you will be able to navigate your way through the world's more widely used computer application for book production. This ebook has literally condensed a course that would cost you several thousand dollars and a week of your time into a simple, direct, turnkey system to get you from manuscript to PDF in a matter of hours. There are no startup costs to do this, and you will be pleased with just how simple it really is to make your own book.

The first thing you need to do is get a copy of Adobe InDesign. The price for the software is quite expensive (about $2,000), but you can try out a fully functional copy of the software for free. Adobe will give you thirty days to try it out; if after thirty days you feel it is a worthy investment to own, there are a few options available to you for purchasing and licensing the software.

You will need to create an Adobe ID account to download the software to your computer. To do this, visit www.adobe.com and click "Sign in" under the search bar in the upper right-hand corner of your screen. On the next screen, click "Don't have an Adobe ID." This will take you to a registration screen where you can choose a username and password.

After you have registered with Adobe and successfully signed into your account, select the "Downloads" tab at the top and then select "Product trials." On the next screen you will see a list of all the Adobe products available for download on a trial basis. Under InDesign, select "Try." This will take you to the InDesign home screen. Then select the "Download trial" button. Again, you will have to make sure that you are signed in with your Adobe ID. Your computer will then walk you through the steps of installing the trial version of Adobe InDesign.

Create a Folder on Your Desktop for Your Book

While this seems like a no-brainer, it's important that you keep track of all the contents of your book in one place. When you are done, you will more than likely have at least four different folders with different files for your book. Name the folder by the book's title, or something that will help you navigate to it later.

Chapter 1: Prepping Your Manuscript

Adobe InDesign lets you import your manuscript directly from Microsoft Word and other word processing programs. There are a few ways to import text into InDesign. However, before you are ready to import text, there are a few things you need to do to prepare your manuscript for layout. These steps will depend on the amount of text and the various other parts of the manuscript you will be laying out with InDesign. Following these steps will save you time later on when you go through your files in InDesign.

1. **Create separate chapter files in Microsoft Word.** If your book is rather lengthy with numerous chapters (over 100 Microsoft Word pages, or over 40,000 words) you will want to create a separate MS Word file for each chapter. Too much content in one file may overload InDesign—the program has been known to crash quite often due to massive amounts of content. Label each file with an easily recognizable name and chapter number (for example, you could create a file for Chapter 1 of your book with the file name Chapter-01.docx, and so on until the end). If you have any front matter (Introduction, Acknowledgements, Contents, etc.) you can lump all of that into one file (Introduction.docx); the same is true of end matter (epilogue, about the author, etc.). Place all the chapter files into your book folder, and create a separate folder within your book folder for your MS Word files (You could call it "MS Word Files").

2. **Delete all images, charts, and special graphics.** Images, charts, and special graphics (including photographs) do not import well into InDesign from word processing programs. For the time being, create a separate folder in your book folder for such content ("Graphics") and place all the original files into that folder. If you are deleting graphics from your MS Word file, you will need to put in some type of placeholder text to let you know that you will need to insert something. Typically, this is done by placing the information in carets <>, and it includes the file name that should be placed, along with any information that might be necessary to remember. For example, if you had a picture on page 3 of your manuscript in Chapter 1 and it was centered, you can enclose the following information in carets: "<insert XYZ-01.jpg, centered>." Place this information in the exact spot where you deleted the original image or graphic. In the Graphics

folder, make sure all the special graphics are labeled accordingly. If you have several images in each chapter, you could label them sequentially (chapter01_im01.jpg, chapter01_im02.jpg).

3. **Delete any special formatting.** InDesign will recognize information from your MS Word document that you have already formatted. These things include boldface type, italics, underlining, small caps, and all caps. For other formatting, such as bullet points, numbered lists, special fonts, callouts, and hyperlinks, it is recommended that you denote special formatting using carets. For example, if you have a numbered list, enter "<numbered list>" before the start of the list and "<end numbered list>" after the list. Another way to do this is to create your own codes, and then use a forward slash (/) to denote the end of a special formatting task. For example, a numbered list could be "nl," so to begin the list you enter "<nl>." To end the list you enter "</nl>."

Chapter 2: Setting Up a Book Template in InDesign

There are a few things you will need to know before you can set up your book template. A template is a file that you will use to design all of your chapters in InDesign. This chapter will cover the basics of setting up a template for a book that is mostly text (a novel, for example). For books that have lots of formatting (different font sizes and types), please consult the advanced edition of *How to Design a Book Using Adobe InDesign*. The screenshots in this ebook are from a Mac version of InDesign. The presentation and shortcuts listed in this ebook will vary depending on your operating system and the version of InDesign you are using.

Define the parts of your book

For most novels, a book is divided into three principle parts: front matter, body, and end matter. In front matter, you will have the title page, a copyright page, and a contents page. You may also have acknowledgements, a dedication, an introduction, or a prologue.

The body is divided into chapters. Typically, there is a chapter heading, followed by body text. There may be subheadings within the body, and perhaps a section that is in a different font than the rest.

The end matter may include an author biography and/or contact info for the author, a glossary, an excerpt from a future book, a list of other books the author has written, or marketing and promotional items.

Create a list of all the key components of your book for each section. Next you will need to determine how many different font styles you plan to use for each section. There is a short guide in the back of this book for recommended font style changes based on section.

Let's say you want to create the most basic book you can, with as few font types used as possible. And let's say that you want to use the same font style for virtually every page in your book. At the very least, you will need a font for your body text (the most important part of the book), a font for your chapter heading, and one for any subheadings that appear in the book. And let's say that you have some section breaks as well (usually centered and may appear as a few dots or an icon of some sort). For your list you would state:

Front matter

    Title page

Copyright page

Contents page

Acknowledgements page

Body

chapter heading

body text

subhead

section breaks

End Matter

Author bio

This list has nine different font (or paragraph) styles. But you could use one for a few of the items in your list. Let's say you choose to use the same font style for your author bio, contents page, and acknowledgements page. That means you have a total of six font styles in your book. Of course, you may choose to use more font styles in your book, or you may have a need to create more varied styles for a special purpose. That's fine. This ebook will provide the basics on how to set up those styles in InDesign so you can create as many as you will need for your book.

Trim Size, Margins, and Gutter Space

Before you can create a page in InDesign for your book, you will need to know its size. Often called the "trim size," this is the size of the book when it is in print. For example, if you want a 6" x 9" book, your trim size is 6 in. by 9 in. The best way to determine your trim size is to contact your printer to see which sizes are available.

For the purposes of this book, let's say you do choose **6" x 9"** as your trim size.

Margins are the white space that appears above, below, and to either side of the printed words. Most printers recommend at least .5" of margin space, but this will depend on anything else you choose to include in that area. For example, if you want to include page numbers and running heads (usually the author's name, book title, or chapter title that appears at the top of each page), you will want to make the margins a bit bigger on the top and bottom. For running heads, factor in at least another .25"; for page numbers that run at the bottom of the page, factor in at least .25". Let's say your book will have running heads at the top of the page, and page numbers at the bottom.

The gutter space is typically the amount of space that exists in the "gutter," or the white space between two pages of an open book. The gutter space will depend heavily on the overall size of your book. For example, if your book is over 100 pages, the gutter space must be wider than 1" (.5" on each page) or you run the risk of the text inching too close to the creases. For the purposes of this book, let's say your book is only seventy-five pages and, thereby, your gutter is only 1" (.5" on each page).

Page Setup

So the book we are creating is seventy-five pages long; it is 6" x 9", with margins at .75" for the top and bottom, .5" for the outside margin, and .5" for the inside margin. We are now ready to create a template for the book.

In InDesign, on the top menu bar, select File>New>Document.

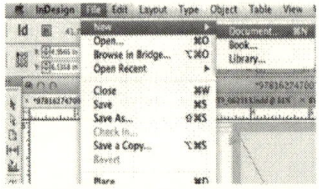

In the "New Document" window, enter in your parameters.

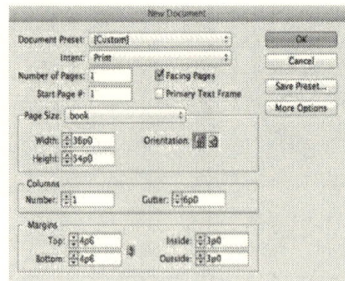

Page Size

> width: 6 in.
>
> height: 9 in.

Columns

> number: 1

gutter: 1 in.

Margins

    top: .75 in.

    bottom: .75 in.

    inside: .5 in.

    outside: .5 in.

    Then click "OK." InDesign will open up a new window with your page based on the dimensions you just created. Save the document as a template by selecting File>Save As. At the bottom of the Save As window, select InDesign Template.

    Create a separate folder in your book folder and call it "InDesign Template."

    Now we're going to define font and heading styles in the template for use in all of the chapters. Return to the list you created earlier of all the possible font styles that will be included in your book. I'm going to show you how to import a chapter from one of your MS Word files to create the styles you need. For example, let's say you want to import Chapter 1 of your book to create these styles.

    On the left-hand side of your InDesign application, you will see a column made up of icons. This is your toolbox panel. Click on the one that looks like a letter "T."

    T.

    Then move your mouse anywhere inside the pink border of your template page. Select Control D (Command D on a Mac)—the shortcut for "Place." This will open up a window to search your computer for files. Navigate to your book folder and then select Chapter 1 from your MS Word files folder. Click "Open."

    Next you will see a new cursor, which looks like it has the first few words of your chapter file in it. Move your cursor to the upper left-hand corner of the pink box.

Then press the Shift key and click your mouse. This will flow in all of the text from that chapter into your InDesign document. You should be able to see the first page of your chapter file in the new page you have created.

Now we are going to define paragraph styles. On the right-hand side of your InDesign window are a series of boxes associated with tasks. Look for the one that says "Paragraph Styles" and click on it.

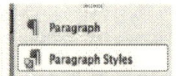

A new window will open to the left of it. At the bottom of that window, look for the icon that looks like a page of book being folded back

A new style (called "Paragraph Style 1" by default) will show up in the list above. Double click on "Paragraph Style 1." A new window will open: Paragraph Style Options.

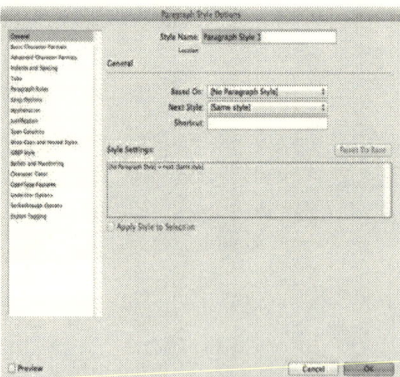

This is your control panel for defining all of your paragraph styles. This ebook will show you how to set up basic paragraph styles. For more advanced information about setting up paragraph styles, consult the advanced version of *How to Design a Book Using Adobe InDesign*.

The first thing you want to do is name your style. Next to "Style Name" enter a name for your first style. Let's say we are designing the paragraphs for your body text. You could name it "body text."

Next, go to the "Basic Character Formats" tab. This is where you will define the font face and size. Under "Font Family," choose from the list of fonts already installed on your computer. For information about how to install fonts on your computer, consult the advanced version of *How to Design a Book Using Adobe InDesign*. If you are not sure what font to use, you can back out of the paragraph style menu by clicking cancel, and then using InDesign's sample font viewer to determine which fonts to use. For the purposes of this book, let's say you have the Palatino font installed on your computer. You would select "Palatino" from the list of fonts.

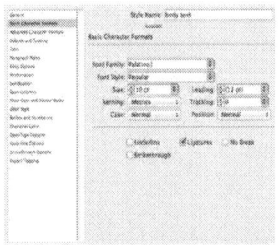

Under "Font Style," choose "Regular." Most font faces have a bold and italic version; some even have variations of these (light, semibold, bold italic, etc.). Since this is the font you will use for the body of your book, you want it to be clear and readable.

Next select the font size. Let's say you are selecting a font size of 10 points for this book. To the right of that is a selection option for something called *leading*. Leading is the space between lines of text in a paragraph. InDesign factors in a default line spacing for you, but you can always add more or less based on your needs. For a font size of 10 points, it automatically selects 12 point. Let's select 11 points for this book.

Then go to the "Indents and Spacing" tab. Most paragraphs have an indent of .25" or more for the first line of text. Also, paragraphs in books tend to be justified, meaning both the left and right margins are flush with the edge of the text area (except for the first line, which will have an indent). Under "Alignment," select "Left Justify." And next to "First Line Indent," enter .25 in. Then press "OK" at the bottom of the window.

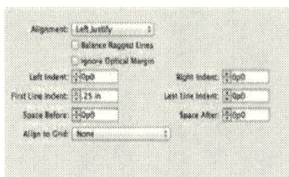

Now, you are going to go back to your page layout and select the first paragraph of text. You can click anywhere within the paragraph (again, make sure that you are using the "T" tool when you select). Then, simply go over to your list of paragraph styles and select the option for "body text." You should now see the paragraph you selected converted to the new style. It should be left justified with a .25" indent for the first line, and the text should be Palatino.

Once you learn how to navigate the New Paragraph window, you can add and delete features anytime you want. The great thing about setting everything up in a template is, if you make any changes to your paragraph styles, they will automatically be reflected for any text within your book which uses that style.

Now let's create a style for your chapter heading. You are basically going to follow the same technique of creating a new paragraph style. This time, name it "chapter heading." Let's say you want to use a new font face for your chapter heading, and that you want it to be centered and appear 1" from the top of the page. You also want a bit of space to appear between the chapter title and the first paragraph.

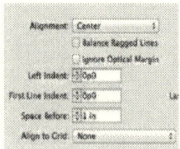

Once you are in the New Paragraph dialogue box, while on the General tab, change the "Based On" dropdown selection to "[No Paragraph Style]." Under the "Basic Character Formats" tab, select a Font Family of "Goudy Old Style." Select the Font Style of "Bold," and the font size as 18. You can leave the leading at the automatic setting. Under the "Indents and Spacing" tab, select "Center" next to Alignment. Under Space Before, enter 1 in. Since you want to have some space between the chapter heading and the paragraph, enter .5 in. under Space After. Then click OK at the bottom of the dialogue box.

Now return to the layout page. Click anywhere in the chapter heading, and then select the "chapter heading" style. You will notice that the chapter heading is now boldface type, Goudy Old Style. There will be a bit of space between the chapter title and the first paragraph. Now go to the beginning of the chapter heading in your page layout and hit the Return key. You should see the title drop down 1 in. on the page.

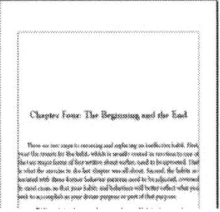 

Continue these exercises for all of the styles you intend to define. Don't worry if you have not defined every style the way you want. You can tweak these files as you go along. But always make sure that you do it in the template file; otherwise, the changes will not be reflected in other files.

The last thing we need to do is create what are called *master pages*. Master pages work like templates within a file. They give you the ability to create pages that can be used as many times as you want within a particular InDesign file. If you recall earlier, we talked about running heads and page numbers. Let's say you want to create a page with a page number that always appears *at the bottom of the page* on the first page of a chapter, and then create running heads with page numbers *at the tops of the pages* for all other information within the chapter. Let's also say that you want to have your name appear on the left-facing page and the title of the book on the right-facing page. We will create one master page for the first page of the chapter, one for the right-facing page, and one for the left-facing page—a total of three pages.

On the tabs at the right-hand side of your InDesign application, you should notice a tab that says "Pages" at the top. When you click on that, you will notice a thumbnail of all the pages in this particular book file. At the very top of that flyout window, you will also see a few sample pages. One is marked "None" and the other is marked "A-Master. Double-click on one of the A-Master thumbnail pages. This should open up a two-page blank document.

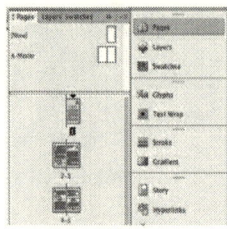

Now we are going to add content to that page that will appear every time we use the A-Master page. For this one, we will simply be adding a page number at the bottom of the page. With the Type tool selected (The "T" from the toolbox on the left side), draw a square box underneath the pink box on the left hand page. You do this by moving the cursor to the upper left-hand corner of where you want the box to appear. Then, holding down the left button on your mouse you drag the cursor to the lower right-hand corner of the box you want to create. Don't worry if it doesn't quite line up where you want; we'll fix that in a minute. You should see a text cursor appear somewhere inside the box.

It might be a good idea to create a style for use within this box. InDesign will automatically try to guess which paragraph style you want to use, and it may not be a good choice. If you don't want to create a new style, simply go to the paragraph styles flyout menu and select "Basic Paragraph" or "No Style." However, in order to get the right font, you will have to go to the control panel at the top to select the font size and other attributes. Make sure the box marked with an "A" is selected in the upper left-hand corner of the control panel—this is so you can adjust fonts. For paragraph adjustments, simply select the paragraph symbol under the "A."

Since you want to use this page for multiple chapters, you don't want to put in an actual page number. You will put in a placeholder, which will automatically tabulate the pages once the book files have been built.

Make sure your cursor is centered within the box you just created (there is a paragraph adjustment tab on the far right of the control panel). Right click on the mouse to open the flyout menu. Select "Insert Special Character" then "Markers" and then "Current Page Number."

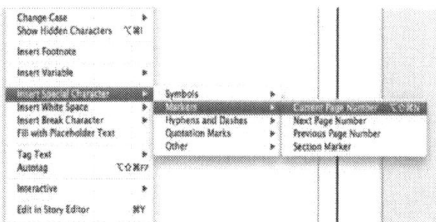

The letter "A" should appear in the box you created. This "A" is a placeholder; anytime you use the A-Master, this "A" will be replaced with the correct page number.

Finally, you will want to duplicate this text box on the right-facing page in the exact same spot. Switch to the Selection tool in your toolbox (the solid arrow that appears at the top of the list). Then click on the box you created on the left-facing page. Do a simple copy and paste (Control C, Control V for PC; Command C, Command V for Mac). Then drag the box to the exact spot on the opposite page so that both pages look identical.

You can also use the Selection tool to edit the size and location of your boxes. This will be covered again in the section on images. Using the selection tool, click on any text box or image box. You will notice tiny squares that appear in the corners of these boxes. Simply click on a tiny box and move the cursor to a new location.

You can use the same techniques to create other master pages. For example, since we want to create a similar page that has the author and title info included, we want to create a new master page and then apply the same techniques. Go back to the pages tab (top selection in right tool bar) and click on the icon that appears in the upper right-hand corner of the flyout menu. Select "New Master" from the menu. In the New Master dialogue box, choose the letter "B" as the prefix and make sure there are two pages.

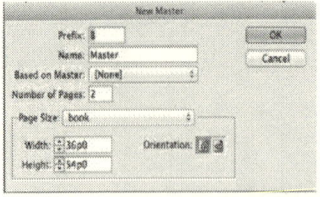

Now you are ready to create the B-Master. Use the same techniques from earlier, but you'll want to add the new written content to the top of the page rather than at the bottom (you can still leave the page numbers at the bottom if you like).

I'll show you how to apply master pages once we have finished creating the template. You're almost ready to start laying out pages in InDesign! The last thing we need to do is delete all the extra pages in the template and delete all the imported text you used to create the paragraph styles.

Click anywhere in the original template document (go to Pages tab and double-click on any of the pages there). Then, using the Type tool from the toolbox, select anywhere within the text. Do a Control/Command A to select all of the text and then press Delete. Then go to the Pages tab once more. Click on page number 2, then scroll down to the end of the document thumbnails and click on the last page while pressing the Shift key. This should select every page except the first one. Then, with your cursor pointed at one of the selected files, hold down the left mouse button and drag the selected file to the trash can in the lower right-hand corner of the flyout menu. Make sure there is no text lingering in this file. Then save your template file once more and close out of it.

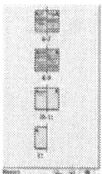

If you need to add or delete any formatting from the template after you have saved it, or if you discover that you are missing a style or two while doing the chapter layouts, you will need to reopen the template file (shows up with a .indt extension in your folder) to make that adjustment. Before you save and close the template file, however, make sure you delete any extra text or pages from the template. Then resave it under the same name, and make sure you select InDesign Template.

Chapter 3: Creating Chapter Files in InDesign

Next we are going to learn how to create chapter files in InDesign. Earlier, I mentioned how InDesign doesn't like files that are very large; creating an entire book in one file can lead to the application not working properly or crashing. Instead, we create chapter files for each chapter in our root word processing program and then use those files to create duplicates in InDesign. Then, as I will show you later, we will put all the files together into a book file that you can edit and rearrange.

From the top navigation menu, select File>Open. Then navigate to the template file you created in your book folder (file will end with .indt). Double-click on the file. When you open the file, it will no longer be in template form. Now you will be able to edit as you see fit. But, the great thing is all of your styles, formatting, and master pages have been saved in this file.

For now, let's skip the front matter section and create the file for Chapter 1. Go to File>Save As, and then create a new folder within your book folder called "InDesign Chapter Files." Save this new file as "Chapter 01.indd" then click OK. Use this same format for all the new chapter files you create. For Front Matter, I generally like to use "Chapter 00.indd" and for end matter "Chapter 99.indd." It will be easier if all the files appear in numerical order in your folder. Later, we will be organizing these files into our InDesign book file.

Now we are going import the text from the Chapter 1 MS Word file. Click on the Text tool in the toolbox, then select anywhere within the pink text box on your page layout. Do a Control/Command D to place the MS Word file. Select the corresponding file in your MS Word book folder (Chapter-01.docx). Then move the cursor to the upper left-hand corner of the pink box, hold down the Shift key, and click your mouse. This should flow all of the text from the Chapter 1 MS Word file into InDesign.

Next you will be applying styles to everything in your layout. Each heading and every ounce of text should have its own style. If there are blank lines or extra spaces, it's a good idea to delete them. If you discover that you need extra space in your formatting, you can always add that into the template. Follow the instructions in Chapter 2 about how to add/delete information to/from the template file.

Now you need to figure out which master pages to use for each layout page. There may be a default master page being used for each new page you have created. If it is A-Master (the double-sided file we created with the page number at the bottom), you will need to use that only for the first page in the file. The other pages will use the B-Master you created in the template. To change those pages to the B-Master, go to the Pages tab and click on page 2 in the thumbnail list. Then scroll down to the last page in the thumbnail list while holding the Shift key. This should select every page except the first one.

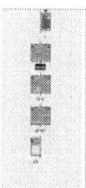

Finally, right-click while the cursor is on one of the selected thumbnail pages. Select B-Master from the dropdown list and click OK. Now all of your pages (beginning with page 2) will use the B-Master.

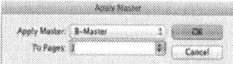

Importing Images, Charts, and Graphs

If you took out any images during the stripping process, you will need to put them back in now. Use the same technique for importing files as you did with text (Control D). First locate the section where you want to place the image. Then using the Text tool, point the cursor in that particular section and do a Control D. You can adjust the size of the file by switching to the Selection tool and then resizing the image by selecting one of the corners. You can also select the entire image (use Text tool, place cursor directly following the image, then hold down the Shift key and use the back arrow on your keypad to select the image; then use the formatting panel at the top to make the image move to center, flush right, or flush left by selecting the appropriate icon; remember also to select [Basic Paragraph] from your Paragraph Style tab to erase any embedded formatting). For more about working with images, see the advanced version of *How to Design a Book Using Adobe InDesign*.

Another thing I recommend doing is anchoring your image files to the text. Click on the little anchor icon that appears at the top of your image and drag it to the end of the paragraph above the image file. This will assure that your image will remain in its exact location if you have to adjust text in your chapter file.

After you have formatted all of the text, there may be some extra pages in your file or there may not be enough pages. To delete pages, simply select them in the pages thumbnail list and drag them to the trash can at the bottom of the flyout menu. To add pages, simply drag the type of page you want to add from your master list and place it next to the last page in the thumbnail list. So, if you need to add one or more B-Master pages, just drag a B-Master page from the master list to the bottom of the thumbnail list. Then navigate to the penultimate page in your file (the page before the one you just placed. You should see a small red box at the end of the text box on that page. Using the Selection tool, click on the red box. The red box will disappear and the cursor will have a few words from your chapter underneath it. Now move the cursor to the top of the fresh page and click the mouse while pressing the Shift key. Pressing the Shift key will assure that all the text will flow onto as many pages as are necessary.

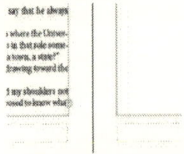

You should now see page numbers on your file pages. Right now they will always begin with the number 1 and then increase sequentially. Later I will show you how to put the chapter files together into a book, which will automatically tabulate the page numbers for you.

Save your chapter file in the InDesign Chapter Files folder for your book. Continue with each chapter until there is an InDesign file for each MS Word file you created.

Now you are ready to design the front matter. Open up a new version of the template you saved, and save it in your InDesign folder as Chapter 00.indd. Use the Control D feature to find the Chapter00.docx file in your MS Word folder and place into InDesign, just like you did with the other chapter files. Then go through and style all of the text within your document. For now, leave the entries on the Contents page blank. I will show you how to create this once the book has been built. Also, make sure that the title page uses the blank master page.

Page Numbering for Front Matter

Most front matter sections have roman numerals instead of Arabic numerals; this typically shows a separation between the front matter and the body. There is simple way to change the contents of your front matter section to roman, as opposed to Arabic, numerals. Go to your pages tab and right-click on the first page in the thumbnails. Then select "Numbering & Section Options." Under Style, select the sequential roman numerals option (i, ii, iii, iv, v...). You should notice that all of the page numbers in this section are now roman numerals.

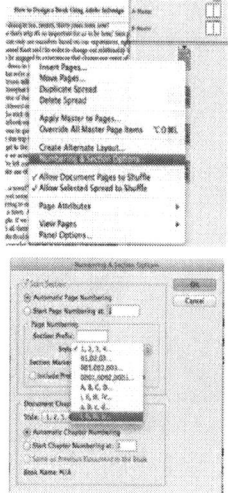

Creating an InDesign Book

Now you are going to compile all the chapters together into a book. The book will automatically tabulate all of the book files for you and assign page numbers for them.

Go to File>New>Book.

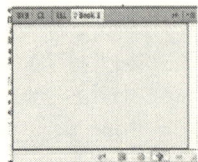

Save the book file in a new folder in your book contents folder on your desktop. Name the file according to your book's title, or something easy to remember. A tab should open on the right-hand side of your InDesign application with the name of your book. Click the plus sign (+) in the lower right-hand corner of that box to add your book files.

Then, navigate to folder where all of your InDesign books are filed. You can select the first file in the folder (should be Chapter 00.indd), and then do a Shift + click on the last file in the folder, and this will select all of the files. Click OK. This will import all of your book files into the Book folder in InDesign.

All of the files should be in order. If they are not, simply drag the file to its proper location. It may take a while for all the files to be organized accordingly, but make sure you do this before moving to the next step. You should notice that the first section (Chapter 00.indd) is listed with roman numerals and the subsequent folders are listed with Arabic numerals. If this is not the case—for the second section, for example—simply open that file and navigate to the Pages thumbnails. Follow the same procedure as was listed above, except this time begin the section with Arabic numerals (1, 2, 3, 4...).

Now you can successfully build your table contents. As I mentioned earlier, there are two ways to do this. The first is simply to go down the list of files in your book list and enter the first number of each section range. Since each chapter is a separate file, InDesign will now tell you which page each section begins on.

The other way is a bit more complex, but if you intend to use this file for anything else besides a printed book (website, ebook), I would recommend getting familiar with this way of creating a contents page. This involves InDesign searching your book files to determine on what page each section begins.

On the top navigation bar, select Layout>Table of Contents... On the next screen choose a title for your contents page (usually "Contents" or "Table of Contents").

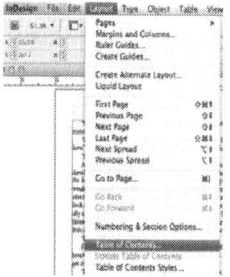

Then, under Styles in the Table of Contents, select the paragraph styles that denote only the beginning of a chapter. If you recall, you created a style called "chapter heading" that was to be used on every chapter heading in your book. Select this style and click "Add."

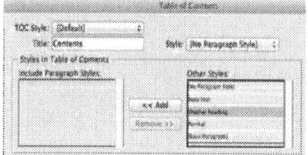

This will add the style to the autogenerated contents page. In the lower section, make sure "Include Book Documents" is selected. This will pull all of the content for which the style "chapter heading" was used and incorporate it into your contents page. Then click OK.

Now InDesign will take you back to your book. On a section outside of your page files (to the right or left of them) click to release the contents of the autogenerated contents page. On the existing contents page, highlight all the content and press delete. Then copy the autogenerated contents and paste into the blank contents page. Style as necessary using the formatting bar at the top of your InDesign program.

Chapter 4: Creating a Print-Ready PDF

Now you are ready to create a PDF for printing. Make sure you check with your printer for any specialized criteria that must be met for print-ready files. This procedure will show you the basics of how to do this.

In your book files panel, select all of the files in your book project (select the first file, then Shift + the last file). Then click the icon in the upper right-hand corner and select "Export Book to PDF" from the flyout menu.

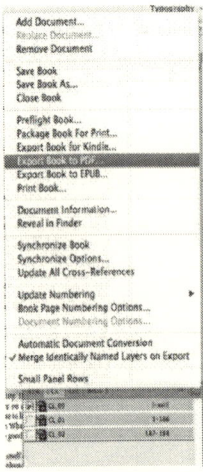

Then, navigate to your book files folder on your desktop. Create a new folder called "PDFs." Choose a new name for the PDF file, or simply use the default one (whatever you named your book). IMPORTANT! Before you click OK, make sure that you select Print PDF and not Interactive PDF at the bottom of the Save As window.

In the new screen that opens, select the type of PDF you want to make. You can select "High-Quality Print" or "Press Quality" unless your printer is more specific about what kind of file it needs to print. Then click OK. InDesign will export your file to a PDF for you in seconds.

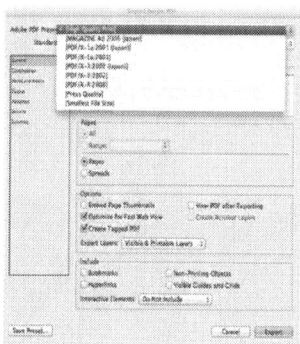

And you're done! If you need to make any changes to your book files, you can simply go into the InDesign files and make the changes. Then, you can save the files again and then export a new version of your book for printing. It's that simple.

The last thing you might want to know is how to export all of your book files for professional use. Say you have created this file and you want to hire someone to make changes to it, or you need to supply all of the root files to your printer for a prepress check. There's a simple way to do this. Simply go to the book files tabs and click on the icon in the upper right-hand corner once more. This time select "Package Book for Print."

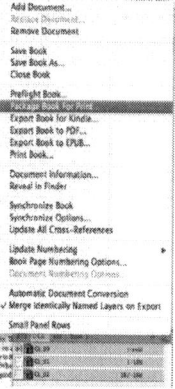

A window will show up, listing all of your fonts, any graphic links, etc. that will be included in the packaged file. Then it will ask you where you want to save this file. You can save it to your book contents files folder on your desktop, but make sure you save it in a new folder.

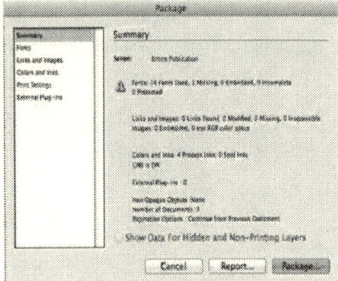

Made in the USA
Monee, IL
11 June 2022

97836773R00016